THE MONEY

POEMS

A SIMPLE PLAN FOR **DAILY ABUNDANCE**

SHERRI JAMES
AND
MARK ALLEN FELTON

THE MONEY POEMS

Published by Mark Allen Felton and Sherri James

Originally published as an eBook ©2009 Mark Allen Felton and Sherri James.

©2017 Mark Allen Felton and Sherri James

International Standard Book Numbers: ISBN-13: 978-1545300756

ISBN-10: 1545300755

Cover Design : Ifedayo Victoria

Interior Book Design : Joy Ajayi (magicpenwriter1@fiverr)

Published and distributed by: Mark Allen Felton and Sherri James

Contents

PREFACE

Thank you for purchasing The Money Poems. This unique set of poems is being made available to you as a tool to put you on a path to financial freedom. The proper use of The Money Poems can quickly bring you an astounding level of monetary good fortune. By reciting The Money Poems daily, you deliberately activate a powerful universal law-the Law of Attraction. Simply stated-what you put out, you will get back. That is the Law!

Earth's crammed with heaven,

And every common bush afire with God;

But only he who sees, takes off his shoes,

The rest sit round it and pluck blackberries.

- Elizabeth Barrett Browning

The Money Poems have one primary task and that is to help you in your quest for economic liberation. Regardless of how things may appear, the atmosphere around you overflows with great abundance; it lacks nothing. And now with The Money Poems, you possess an effective tool to convert that plentiful energy into usable, physical wealth.

With daily use of The Money Poems, you will tremendously increase your receptivity to financial resources intended just for you. By simply reciting the poem of the day as often as you like throughout the day, you will strengthen your connectivity to your natural inheritance.

We suggest you memorize the poems, and when a financial challenge arises—recite the poem of the day silently to yourself. Then return to your work more relaxed and focused, knowing that you have dealt with this challenge at the deepest level possible—in your subconscious mind.

Why poems? Research has shown that the imagery associated with poems connects with the innermost part of us, going beyond our conscious awareness into our subconscious mind. Poems penetrate our souls in the same way that music connects with us. Think about it: many songs originate from poems.

Long after we've recited a poem, the imagery from it stays with us, creating extremely powerful, positive impressions in our minds. Those impressions then act as a foundation from which we make every decision.

One of the oldest forms of literature known to mankind, poetry exists in all cultures. Every sacred text—including the Bhagavad-Gita, the Qu'ran, the Holy Bible, and the Tao—contains an abundance of poetry. Some scholars believe poetry may have predated literacy and served as a chief form of communication.

The English word poem derives from the Greek word *poiema*, which means "to make." A poem is a made thing-a creation. The twentieth-century American poet William Carlos Williams referred to a poem as a "machine made of words." We all know that machines are meant to accomplish a task. They do whatever the maker has created them to do. The same is true for this machine made of words, The Money Poems, which you now hold in your hands.

At first glance, The Money Poems seem simple and they are. But, it is their simplicity that quickens the process of converting the lavish, abundant energy around you into usable wealth in all forms.

The more you use The Money Poems, the more open you become to the abundance of the universe. The Money Poems can only work if you work them. Your riches await you!

THE MONEY POEMS

INTRODUCTION

My name is Denise Allen, and I'm the curator of The Money Poems. This is not my real name as I wish to remain anonymous and have changed my name and the names of my family members to protect their privacy.

My family has used The Money Poems for many years. Because of these poems, we have humbly enjoyed a level of financial freedom that most people only get to dream of. With this easy-to-use set of universal instructions, we have created generational wealth that can now be passed on through our family for years to come.

To whom much is given, from him much is required.

In the past, we interpreted the above statement to mean giving charitably and being responsible for each other as a family. Over the years, we've matured in our thinking and come to realize that this statement means to serve all mankind. And in consideration of the world's present economic state, we feel there is no greater time than now to share with you The Money Poems.

For quite some time, The Money Poems have brought our family such great financial freedom. We feel it would be a grave injustice not to share this wonderful gift with the world. My sincerest hope is that The Money Poems have the same effect on you and yours as they have had on us. They changed our lives. I know they can change your life, too.

MY STORY – PART I

Please allow me to share with you my story and how The Money Poems were introduced to me. I was born the middle child of seven children. I have three magnificent older brothers and three charming younger sisters. We are a very close-knit family. Growing up, we didn't always possess many material things, but we've always had each other.

The matriarch of our family was my paternal grandmother, affectionately known as Grandma Ellie to my brothers and sisters and me. Grandma Ellie was one of the wisest people I have ever known. Even until she took her last breath, Grandma Ellie's mind was as sharp as a tack.

Throughout the years, Grandma Ellie would share many stories with us about her life. As a young adult, she lived a very wealthy lifestyle. She often showed us clippings from different magazines of her day. The society pages of those magazines were filled with pictures of Grandpa and her attending swanky events. What an exciting life she led!

As I grew older, I began to wonder what happened to those good old days that Grandma Ellie spoke of so fondly. What happened to the money she often talked about? It was very obvious even to my young mind that things were very different than they used to be. I often wondered, "If Grandma Ellie once had all this money, why is our family struggling so hard financially now?"

So, one day while having lunch with her, I mustered up the courage to ask, "Grandma Ellie, what happened to the good old days? Why doesn't our family have any money anymore? Why are we so poor when you and Grandpa had so much money before?"

Grandma Ellie didn't immediately respond; she just blankly stared out of the window and seemed to ignore my question. I thought to myself, maybe I've asked something that I shouldn't have asked. But, then she suddenly broke her trance and looked at me softly, smiled, and said, "Denise baby, money comes to those who know how to manifest it."

Manifest it! I had no idea what Grandma Ellie could possibly mean. How do you manifest money? When I asked her for more information, she'd just say, "A poem a day brings money your way." I must admit that her reply made me even more confused. It seemed as though she wasn't telling me something; I could see it in her eyes.

No matter how I presented my question, she'd always respond in the same way: "A poem a day brings money your way." Eventually, I gave up asking. But secretly, I hoped to one day solve this riddle of Grandma Ellie's.

Years had passed by and one day I did just that. Grandma Ellie's "riddle" became quite clear. It didn't happen all at once, but in a most unexpected way. It was the spring of my junior year in high school. I was in the middle of tryouts for my high school's cheerleading squad when the Principal came into the auditorium looking for me. I had an urgent phone call awaiting me in her office.

Immediately, I knew something was terribly wrong. In all my years in grade school, I'd never received a call that had to be taken in the Principal's office. As soon as

I picked up the phone, I could hear my mother sniffling. "Denise, you have to come home, baby. Something's happened to Grandma Ellie." I panicked.

The next few hours were a blur. One of my teachers rushed me home in her car. We pulled up to find a ton of activity going on outside our modest home. There was an ambulance by the curb, along with various family members. Suddenly, paramedics rushed frantically from inside wheeling a gurney with Grandma Ellie on it. I jumped out of the car in a frenzied state and ran to the ambulance to find out what happened.

The Emergency Medical Technicians held me back as they shut the door and drove away with my beloved Grandma Ellie inside. My father quickly gathered our family together, and we piled into our wood-paneled station wagon and wildly took off behind the ambulance. We arrived at the hospital, only to sit worriedly in the waiting room, hoping for the best.

Finally, a doctor came out to talk to us. Grandma Ellie had suffered a massive heart attack and they weren't sure if she was going to make it through the night. There was an eerie silence that swept the room.

Gratefully and fortunately for all of us, Grandma Ellie did survive but she would never be the same. All her life, she'd been very independent. Up until that point, I couldn't ever remember thinking of her as being old. She was always so young in spirit that I never thought about how old she might have been. But, this heart attack changed everything. A different reality sunk in.

Soon after, she came to live with us permanently. My brothers and sisters and I took turns caring for her. It's a good thing there were seven of us as we each were assigned a day of the week to care for her. My day was Sunday. My oldest brother, Greg, had Thursday. John, who was just under Greg, had Tuesday. Randy had Saturday. Shelly had Monday. Karen had Wednesday. And Julie, the baby, had Friday. It worked out perfectly.

Grandma Ellie didn't talk as much as she used to, but I always had the feeling there was something she wanted to share with us, and more specifically, with me. She seemed to be looking for some way to do that. One Sunday while I was cleaning her room, Grandma Ellie beckoned me to her bedside and pressed a worn piece of paper into my hand.

Without saying anything, she looked deeply into my eyes and just smiled. I knew whatever she was giving me must have been extremely important, and it felt like something I should cherish. I stuffed the paper into my pants pocket and returned to my chores.

Later when I was alone, I pulled the worn piece of paper from my pocket and began to read it. To my surprise, it was a simple poem. It had a cute little rhyme to it, and although not very long, it seemed to speak volumes. At the time, I had no clue about the poem's value and power. Later, I would come to know that poem as being the Sunday money poem.

I was so happy and loved that Grandma Ellie had given me a poem for the day of the week that I was responsible for taking care of her. It felt like we had our own special bond.

I decided to keep my poem a secret so that my other brothers and sisters wouldn't become jealous of our relationship. In my mind, I was clearly her favorite. As I do today, I would carry my poem with me everywhere I went. Soon after that glorious day, Grandma Ellie would pass away. This triggered a deep sadness in our family. We loved her so much and would miss her dearly. She was such a proud woman and always wanted the best for us.

On many occasions and often to our discomfort, she would speak of a great monetary inheritance that awaited us. We would always try to silence her as no one wanted to imagine what life would be like without her. Upon her passing, none of us had any expectation of any monetary inheritance. We were quite content with all the many cherished memories she left us with.

As time went on, things got pretty rough for our family. My parents had to sell most of Grandma's belongings to cover all her past medical expenses. Besides a few pictures and some other artifacts, there weren't many physical items left of Grandma Ellie's. The simple poem she once gave me now took on an even greater significance; it was the only physical thing I personally had left of hers. I would read it often, and it would give me great comfort. It was my way of staying connected to Grandma Ellie.

MY STORY – PART II

A year after Grandma Ellie left us, I graduated from high school and went away to college. Of course, I carried my poem with me and read it whenever I missed her or just needed to feel better. During my first two years in college, there were two things that happened which changed how I viewed the precious poem Grandma Ellie had given me.

The first incident occurred during the end of my first year. Being the fourth of seven children, I had little money available to me to pay for my college education. My parents were pretty tapped out financially when it was my turn to go to college. Nonetheless, I was determined to attend college, and not just any old college, but an Ivy League school. It didn't matter that I didn't have Ivy League money. I was driven. I applied, and because of my grade point average, I was accepted. In addition, I received a small scholarship.

When I entered college in 1988, I arrived with precious few belongings but a conviction that I would complete my education no matter what. Back home, my parents worried incessantly that I would be sent home for lack of money. That first year was pretty tough. Many of my classmates who had all been educated at boarding schools or overseas or both seemed to be rolling in money, while I obviously struggled. But that didn't matter to me because here I was, at this prestigious university, being educated alongside the sons and daughters of senators, congressmen, and business tycoons, and yet I was holding my own. I had never experienced anything like that before. Although quite intimidating, I enjoyed every moment.

In my first year, my scholarship covered most of my basic expenses, but not all. I still had a balance due to the university. I had no clue how I was going to pay it. I just knew that I couldn't ask my parents for any money. My three younger siblings would soon be attending college, and they would need every penny to help them along their way. Besides, I didn't want to be any more of a burden than I had been already. Yet, if I couldn't pay this balance, I would have to stay home the following year. My dream of graduating from an Ivy League school seemed to be evaporating right before my eyes.

I was in and out of the financial aid office so often that my counselor knew me by name. I had already been granted the maximum amount of aid for my family's financial scenario. Determined to make it, I spent hours in the library during my second semester, researching scholarships and grants. Unfortunately, everything I found was for students just leaving high school or students heading to graduate school.

It seemed I had no options, and I was at my wit's end. I didn't want to go back to my counselor to ask for more money, but I also didn't want to sit out a year because of money, or worse, change schools.

So reluctantly, I set yet another meeting with my financial aid counselor. He had done so much for me, already. I didn't really know what another meeting could accomplish. I just knew that I didn't want to be told that I couldn't come back the following year.

As I was headed to his office, I had this overwhelming feeling of Grandma Ellie's presence. Out of a natural reaction, I suddenly reached for my purse to retrieve the priceless poem she had given me. Grandma Ellie's poem had always been a source of comfort, which is exactly what I needed at that moment. I read it slowly, and as usual, it gave me such a consoling feeling to speak those words. I just felt like everything was going to be alright.

Then like out of a fairy tale book, the unexpected happened. My meeting with my counselor played out like a dream coming true. He had been preparing to tell me that I would not be able to return to school the following fall because of my past due balance. But right before I walked into his office, he received a phone call from an alumnus of the university who wanted to offer a supplemental scholarship to a deserving student with good grades.

It just so happened my grades were impeccable that year, and my counselor felt that I was the perfect candidate to receive this scholarship. Coincidently, the amount of the scholarship was exactly the amount of money I needed to meet the monetary shortage from my first year. I was overwhelmed. My counselor was astonished at the turn of events and happily awarded me the alumnus' gift. Amazingly, I was able to return to school the following fall.

Just as extraordinary, the second curious incident happened at the beginning of the second semester of my sophomore year. After paying off the balance of my tuition, I ended up running through the money I'd saved up over the summer working odd jobs and didn't have enough to purchase all the textbooks I needed for the second school semester. I sat in my dorm room very frustrated. Here I go again.

How would I get through this school year if I couldn't afford the books I needed for class? It just didn't seem fair. Everyone else seemed to be enjoying school, while I struggled to stay afloat. Maybe I was wrong to think I could graduate from such a prestigious university.

As I sat on my dorm bed feeling sorry for myself, I began rummaging nervously through my purse for a piece of gum. My fingers ran across the familiar worn page of Grandma Ellie's poem. Feeling sentimental, I pulled it out and read it aloud a few times. I needed comforting and the poem had always given me that. I wasn't expecting anything to happen as I read it, only to feel comforted. But as I was leaving my dorm room, I suddenly had the thought to contact my department's administrator.

It seemed like such an odd thought because I had few interactions with her, and I couldn't think of one reason as to why I'd need to call her. What would I talk about? So, I just blew it off.

Classes soon began, and I still didn't have the books I needed. Once again, I knew I couldn't call on my parents. So, I tried borrowing my classmates' books, whenever they weren't using them, but that became very challenging because, of course, they needed their own books for class.

What was I to do? I'd found money to stay in school, but now my grades were in danger if I couldn't find money to get the books I needed for my classes. If I didn't find a solution soon, I might be going back home for an entirely different reason. Then, the strangest thing happened again. One afternoon during the third week of classes, I bumped into my department's administrator. I had completely forgotten the thought I'd had a few weeks earlier of contacting her.

We chatted lightly, said our goodbyes, and as I was walking away from her, she paused and asked me if there was anything I needed. Without thinking, I blurted out in a joking voice, "Got any textbooks I can borrow?" As I realized what I'd said, I was immediately flushed with embarrassment. That was a secret that I had been keeping to myself all semester. I had too much pride to tell anyone about my situation.

Fortunately for me, her response quickly put my shame to rest. She asked, "Which books do you need? Maybe I can help you." After pausing for a moment, I sheepishly told her I needed textbooks for all of my classes. And without the slightest hesitation, she sent me straight to the school's bookstore to purchase every book I needed, plus school supplies, all charged to her departmental account. I was flabbergasted! I never imagined something this amazing happening for me.

I promised to pay her back as soon as I could. She wasn't having any of that. She told me the books and supplies were a gift that didn't have to be repaid. But if I felt the need to give back, I could volunteer a few hours in her office when my schedule permitted. Now, I believed in people having good fortune, but these two incidents seemed to go beyond general good fortune.

The solutions to my challenges seemed so tailor made. Was it the poem that assisted me? Could it be? I began to think about the common denominator in both situations and realized it must be. It had to be the poem. In my heart,

I always knew Grandma Ellie had given me something special and that something special was now connected to two seemingly miraculous events in my life.

That day, I committed my poem to memory and recited it for every financial situation that I encountered. The results were always surprising. I was on to something. I made it through college, despite the appearance of limited financial resources.

MY STORY – PART III

After I received my degree in 1992, I went to visit my oldest brother, Greg. He had just opened his own law practice and was struggling with his new business. I was hoping to intern with him while I figured out what I was going to do with the rest of my life. We arranged to discuss my internship over lunch. When I arrived at his office, he was still on a morning conference call that was running long. Always a go-getter, Greg never ceased to impress me. I was proud of him for making the leap to start his own practice. That took a lot of guts.

As I waited for Greg to finish his call, I studied his small office. On the wall, he proudly displayed his diplomas for undergrad and law school. He'd even framed the letter informing him he'd passed the bar exam. The table across from Greg's desk was crowded with framed photos of our family-Greg's graduation from law school, my first game as a cheerleader, John's saxophone solo in front of the mayor, and much more.

As I scanned his office, one particular photo caught my eye. It was a picture of my Grandma Ellie and Grandpa dancing at a posh event. They were dressed in formal attire. I recognized it as one of the clippings Grandma Ellie had shared with us when she was alive.

Seeing that photo reminded me of afternoons with Grandma Ellie, listening to fascinating stories from her youth. Those were the days. I hadn't seen that picture in years.

I picked up the framed clipping to get a closer look, and as I did, a worn piece of paper gently floated from the back of the frame. As soon as I saw it, I knew it was from Grandma Ellie because it looked identical to the piece of paper she'd given me. Was it another poem? My heart raced. Could it be? I knew the miraculous way my poem had been working in my life; the very idea that another poem like it existed was overwhelmingly exciting.

I quickly put the frame down and picked up the paper to read it. To my utter delight, it was another money poem. I was lost for words. I felt a slight knot in my stomach. In all these years, it never occurred to me that Grandma Ellie might have given a poem to any of my siblings.

Over lunch, Greg told me that Grandma Ellie gave him the poem just before she passed away. Like me, he held onto his poem because it reminded him of the days they had spent together. Thursday was Greg's day. He shared with me that he used the poem for emotional support and especially when faced with tough financial situations, oftentimes with unbelievable results. And he, too, thought that he was the only one that Grandma Ellie had given a poem to.

It had been years since Grandma Ellie had passed, but that day she didn't feel so far away. To the contrary, she felt very much alive. Greg and I talked for hours that afternoon, swapping stories of how our poems had worked in our lives. At one point, I'm not sure who said it, but we wondered whether Grandma Ellie had given poems to the others. And, if she had, how had their poems worked for them, too? We would soon find out.

Every Sunday, my brothers and sisters and I got together at my parents' home for a huge family dinner. No one ever missed the big meal. It was our opportunity to catch up on family business. All of my older siblings—except for Greg—were married with children. So Sunday dinner conversations usually focused upon the latest happenings with the grandkids.

I knew that the next Sunday dinner would be completely different. Greg and I agreed to wait until then to tell our siblings about our poems and to ask if they were given poems as well. I bubbled with anticipation the whole week. Finally, Sunday arrived and for the life of me, I cannot remember what we ate that night. I can only remember thinking of all the endless possibilities. It was an electric evening.

After dinner, Greg and I called everyone into the living room. We had a big announcement to make, which got everyone excited! As the whole family listened, I told them about my breathtaking experience at Greg's office and how I'd discovered a special poem given to Greg by Grandma Ellie and that she had given me one, too.

I shared with them how we had each been using the poems in our lives, and how it had never occurred to us that Grandma Ellie might have given a poem to anyone else other than ourselves — how neither of us had ever spoken to one another about our poems because we felt it may stir up jealousy among family members — and how both Greg and I secretly thought we were each Grandma Ellie's favorite. Everyone like clockwork curiously broke into a subdued laughter.

I continued sharing stories that I thought only I knew, but to my surprise, everyone seemed to be familiar with. The more I talked, the louder the laughter became until everyone was in hysterics. I couldn't help but to ask what was so funny? They continued to laugh for several minutes until the laughter finally subsided, and we began to talk amongst ourselves. We discovered that each one of us thought we were Grandma Ellie's favorite. The joke was on all of us; the truth is that she loved us all equally.

As Greg and I continued to share what our poems meant to us individually, my brothers and sisters, one by one, began to pull familiar worn pieces of paper from their wallets and purses. The room went utterly silent, and we just looked at each other in awe! Grandma Ellie had given each of us a poem for the day of the week that we were assigned to take care of her.

We all kept the poems to ourselves because of the same reason. As we gathered the pieces of paper on the coffee table, the profundity of the moment hit us all. No one spoke a word.

We'd always heard of this great inheritance Grandma Ellie had for us, but never believed that it really existed. Now, to our amazement, right here, on the coffee table in front of us were seven powerful poems. Here was her legacy! These poems were our inheritance!

I glanced at my dad who had tears streaming from his eyes. I'd never ever seen my dad cry. He rose from his seat, and through his tears, he explained that it was time he told us the truth about Grandma Ellie and the poems. Anxiously, we all sat forward in our seats, eager to hear about this incredible woman who'd meant so much to us and to our family and these mysterious poems.

Daddy began to unfold a fabulous story of how our beloved Grandma Ellie and Grandpa were extremely wealthy and moved in only the most elite social circles of their time. The clippings Grandma Ellie shared with us when she was alive were but a mere glimpse of a life filled with riches.

As Daddy spoke, I couldn't help but to interrupt and ask the one question that I'm sure was on everyone's mind. "Daddy, if we come from money, what happened to it?"

MY STORY – PART IV

My dad glanced briefly toward my mom. They seemed to make some silent agreement before he continued speaking.

"When my dad died, he left Grandma Ellie an estate valued at over $2.5 million dollars." He paused while we took in this incredible information. He then continued, "You haven't heard me talk much about my older brother, Aaron. Aaron was a free spirit, and as a young adult, he stayed in trouble. He had a sense of entitlement and felt he could do anything without having to pay the price for it. Growing up, we'd both witnessed how our parents used the poems to build our family's wealth. And because of this Aaron seemed to think that we were of a higher class and everyday rules didn't apply to us, or more specifically, to him."

We all knew my dad had an older brother, but we never knew much about him growing up. Now, we knew why. It now made sense why daddy always taught us to love all people equally and that there was nothing magical about being rich. He continued the story but we could sense that it hurt to speak about these old memories.

"Aaron's attitude got him into one mess after another. With every catastrophe, mama would come to his rescue. Eventually, he got into such trouble that mama had to get a lien against our house to bail him out. Aaron promised to be responsible for the house note, but when he skipped town without notice, mama lost the house. That incident drained her financially, and we haven't seen Aaron since. I guess he felt that the wealth had been created so easily that she would just magically recreate it again."

Daddy continued, "Your grandmother and grandfather were partners in every sense of the word. Mama had been an instrumental partner for Grandpa in building our family's wealth. They did it together. I've known about these poems since I was a little boy. They're called The Money Poems. I saw mama and daddy use them all the time.

Mama tried to give the poems to me when I became an adult, but I refused. Aaron's behavior disgusted me so much I didn't want to have anything to do with them. I'd seen how much his arrogance hurt my parents, and I knew I didn't want that in my life. So, I chose to raise you more modestly and that meant without The Money Poems."

"Mama didn't agree with my perspective but she respected my wishes to raise my family the way I wanted to. She wanted to share The Money Poems with you for quite some time, but I refused to let her. That all changed after her heart attack. She and I had a long talk." Grandma Ellie had explained to Daddy that her constantly bailing Aaron out was something she felt she had to do, and she would have done the same for him. How she loved them both unconditionally and wanted the best for them.

She expressed how important it was for her to leave us something and persuaded Daddy to let her share the poems with us. He agreed under the condition that each child would receive only one poem each. And she couldn't tell us how to use the poem or that she'd given a separate poem to each of us. If we discovered that fact on our own, so be it. But, in accordance with Daddy's wishes, it had to be our own discovery.

Daddy knew the power of The Money Poems when

used in combination. And he was painfully aware of the responsibility that unlimited wealth would demand of us. One poem used alone would help us, but the seven poems used together would change our financial picture forever. He was highly concerned about us respecting the enormous wealth that The Money Poems would inevitably bring.

We all sat captivated as Daddy told us of how Grandma Ellie and Grandpa used The Money Poems to create astounding wealth for themselves. Daddy wasn't exactly sure where the poems originated, but he remembered hearing stories from his parents of ancient mystic tales. They seemed to be passed down through generations of our family because they were written on pieces of paper that seemed to be very old from the start.

Daddy told us how in the beginning Grandma Ellie and Grandpa spoke one of the poems aloud to each other every day, and then they would go about their day as normal. At first, nothing seemed to change. In fact, things actually seemed to get worse. But every time a financial issue arose, such as a bill collector calling, Grandma Ellie took the call, dealt with it, and then as soon as she got off the phone, she recited a poem from her collection. Then, she continued with her day as if that phone call had never happened. This continued for some time.

Grandma Ellie often read a poem aloud, never paying much attention to what day each poem represented. Then one day for no particular reason, she began to use the poems as they were prescribed-Monday's poem for Monday, Tuesday's poem for Tuesday, and so forth. That's when things started to change. The change was gradual at first—maybe a little extra food in the pantry or a nice bowtie for Grandpa on a special occasion.

Eventually, the good things began to happen more often, and soon everything began to look different. Grandma Ellie and Grandpa were very happy. Whenever something really, really good would happen financially, they'd look at each other and say,

"A poem a day brings money my way."

How many times had I heard Grandma Ellie say that? And now, I finally understand what she'd meant by it.

The poems used together act like a converter, transforming the abundant energy around us into usable forms. It seems like magic, but it isn't. It is simply using one of the most powerful forms of communication—poems—to seize the energy that surrounds us all day, every day. Riddle solved.

From that day on my brothers and sisters and I resolved to use the poems just as Grandma Ellie and Grandpa used them, and we promised Daddy to respect the good that we knew would come our way. My youngest sister, Julie, collected each of the poems from us and put them into a small book that she distributed throughout the family.

From that day to this one, we've each spoken these poems aloud to ourselves, to one another, and to our families. And just like Grandma Ellie did when she was faced with a bill collector (or another seemingly pressing financial issue), we dealt with the problem, and when we were done, we read the poem of the day to ourselves and returned to our day more focused and relaxed, as if it never happened.

Our lives have changed so dramatically since that incredible Sunday. All of us are now millionaires. Greg's law practice became one of the city's largest firms. My brother John has toured all over the world as a premier saxophonist. Randy is a physician with a booming practice. Shelly and Karen both own more than $25 million in real estate each. And Julie, the baby, has a string of successful daycare centers. As for me, I've been developing charter schools to help kids in poor communities excel academically.

The Money Poems have done so much good for my family. It's been an amazing journey. It's time to share this secret with the world! I now understand clearly why Grandma Ellie gave me the poem about serving. She knew this information needed to serve more than just our family, and I would take on that responsibility of doing so. That was what she was trying to communicate to me so intensely back then. I finally got it. So, it is with great pleasure that I present to you The Money Poems.

Remember, a poem a day brings money your way!

DENISE ALLEN

THE MONEY POEMS

SUNDAY

~Sharing~

My money grows from a seed, which is planted in
my mind,

A seed watered with belief, feeling, and time.

I have learned I must give to receive.

This universal law I always will believe.

Every day presents an opportunity to plant a seed,

A seed that can grow to fulfill my every need.

I plant into the lives of others as I plant into mine,

When I pray for the best for all mankind.

Serving is the word that covers this precious day.

I am truly grateful for what is known as
Sharing Sunday.

A POEM A DAY BRINGS MONEY MY WAY!

MONDAY

~Fruitful~

I learn to love that which I cannot see

For these invisible thoughts bring unseen fortunes
to me.

I catch the vision, which lives in my mind,

Knowing that it will manifest in due time.

The invisible soon comes to light,

Raising my status to a brand new height.

I gather all the seeming impossibilities,

And with right thought, turn them into living realities.

These thoughts I have on this precious day,

The beginning of the week, Fruitful Monday.

TUESDAY

~Plentiful~

Today, I rise above all money woes.

I feel prosperous from my head to my toes.

As I move gracefully through this wonderful day,

My finances grow in every single way.

I embrace the harmony of my fabulous life.

I release all my worries and all of my strife.

The universe responds to my words like a child,

Fulfilling all my desires and doing it now.

I am thankful for this knowledge, this glorious day,

As I continue my week on Plentiful Tuesday.

WEDNESDAY

~Abundant~

As the rising sun emits rays of light,

I am reminded of the blessings within my sight.

These blessings rain down on me through the clouds,

Cleansing all my mistakes, so that I stand tall,
head unbowed.

Ideas of plenty penetrate my mind's soil,

Growing to heights that are reserved for the royal.

My path is lit by the perfect light,

A light that always burns through the day and
the night.

The middle of the week is what they call this day,

I like to call it Abundant Wednesday.

THURSDAY

~Resourceful~

Money comes to me by the command of my voice.

It does so because it has no choice.

This ability is the result of universal law,

A law written not for one, but for all.

What I speak with my tongue comes into fruition.

So, I speak wealth into my life to uplift my condition.

My words are spoken with unwavering finality,

Causing my world to reflect its new prosperous reality.

I know the power of my words, so I speak with
careful precision,

And on this Resourceful Thursday, I solidify
my position.

FRIDAY

~Harvest~

Today, I continue the mental conditioning that brings
me wealth.

With every thought I think, I create lasting
financial health.

My precious thoughts easily take on desirable form.

Living a successful life has quickly become my norm.

Now that I have reconnected with the universe,

I feel that I have thrown off a longstanding curse.

What a difference I see since I changed my
mind's direction.

No longer financially lacking, wealth is my
permanent reflection.

The eagle flies on this transitional day,

A day known to all as Harvest Friday.

SATURDAY

~Thankful~

Like a flower, my finances grow with such
stunning beauty.

This expansion occurs naturally because I fulfilled my
personal duty.

Every day I let go of hoping for the manifest of
empty wishes;

Instead, I reaffirm that I am the rightful heir of
infinite riches,

Now that I have released thoughts of limitation,

I have thrown the door wide open for
unlimited creation.

Thoughts of plenty lead to actions that quickly take
me higher.

My mind is now clear for the realization of my
deepest desires.

I feel renewed and refreshed as I go on my way,

Carrying with me a mindset of completion on
Thankful Saturday.

A POEM A DAY BRINGS MONEY MY WAY!

THE POWER OF THE SPOKEN WORD

The rain and snow come down from the heavens

and stay on the ground to water the earth.

They cause the grain to grow, producing seed for the

farmer and bread for the hungry.

It is the same with my word.

I send it out, and it always produces fruit.

It will accomplish all I want it to,

and it will prosper everywhere I send it.

-Isaiah 55:10-11

THE MONEY POEMS 2017

Wow! Mark and I first wrote The Money Poems in 2008. It's now nine years later. I'm a minister, and Mark travels the world supporting himself through his music!

In the last nine years, I have invested considerable time in understanding how consciousness is built and how to teach others to do it. This edition is the result of that work. We added these final chapters to the original publication to show you how to put The Money Poems into action. As my spiritual mother and teacher, Rev. Della, would say, "You cannot do what you do not understand." We want you to understand why The Money Poems work and how to make them work for you.

"By faith we understand that … what is seen was made from the things that are not visible" (Hebrews 11:3). Like invisible cars traveling back and forth across the border between the seen and the unseen worlds, your words move between the visible and the invisible, bringing you experiences and conditions to match the quality of the words you speak. The Money Poems System shows you how to methodically and intentionally send the right "vehicles" across the border.

The spoken word can be audible or inaudible. Do not just watch what you say aloud; watch what you say in your head, too. *This inner chatter escapes the observation of most people, and it is your consciousness.* It is the driver of your actions and the captain of your ship. In fact, if I could follow you all day with a recorder and capture all that you say and think, it would no longer surprise you why your day may often go south.

Listen to what Neville Goddard says about this inner chatter: "Your inner speech is perpetually written all around you in happenings ... By inner speech is meant those mental conversations which you carry on with yourself. They may be inaudible when you are awake because of the noise and distractions of the outer world ... but they are quite audible in deep meditation and dream. But whether they be audible or inaudible, you are their author and fashion your world in their likeness."

The Money Poems System shows you how to take control of your outer and inner speech. By following a few simple techniques, you will be able to harness this creative power. Used faithfully over time, this system cannot fail to produce abundance in your life.

One more thing before we close this chapter ... Do your abundance work!

Doing your job is not the same thing as doing your abundance work. Becoming excellent in your work will not eliminate your responsibility to become excellent in your mind. You must carve out a definite time to study wealth and prosperity, deal with your money psychology, and expand what you think is financially possible for you.

Unaddressed financial stress does not go away; it simply changes form. Fears about money do not evaporate as income increases. Poor money habits do not correct themselves. Unchecked greed grows. You must set aside a definite time each day to work on your beliefs about money. You must consciously open the door for money while simultaneously closing it on lack and limitation.

Who you are with five cents is who you will be with five million ... *unless* you do your abundance work!

THE MONEY POEMS SYSTEM

Wealth includes so much more than money. Financial wealth held in the absence of peace, joy, happiness, good relationships, and satisfying work, is no wealth at all. When you do your abundance work, you set up your mind to attract wealth in all forms.

Money flows freely to the one whose mind invites prosperity. The Money Poems System develops the mind in you that makes financial wealth inevitable. Each time you recite one of the poems, you till the soil of your mind, making it more and more receptive to plenty in all forms.

It is our inner conversations which make tomorrow's facts.

-Neville Goddard

Many people talk money away from themselves through negative self-talk. The Money Poems System helps you stop this crippling habit once and for all by giving you the right inner conversation for wealth. If you will let it, The Money Poems System can permanently and positively change your inner conversation about money.

The Money Poems System is the secret to making the poems work. By themselves, The Money Poems can bring *temporary* relief. A poem recited every now and again can produce some wonderful manifestations. But if you want to be changed at depth, if you want a new attitude about money, then you want to master The Money Poems System.

The Money Poems System is simple:

1. Recite the poem of the day with feeling 7 times during the day. You can do it all at once, or you may spread it out throughout the day. It does not matter.

2. Keep this habit for 7 weeks and track your progress using The Money Poems Tracker at the end of this book.

3. Journal for 2 minutes daily on any insights that come up for you during this process.

4. At the end of the 7 weeks, assess your progress.

5. Repeat.

WHAT MAKES THE MONEY POEMS SYSTEM WORK

Working The Money Poems System will not be hard. Getting started will not take much. What will challenge you is remaining consistent. Following through until your mind changes ... well, that's the difference between success and failure.

There are four principles upon which The Money Poems System is built: (1) autosuggestion, (2) intensity of feeling, (3) persistence, and (4) gratitude.

AUTO-SUGGESTION

Napoleon Hill explains auto-suggestion in his classic book *Think and Grow Rich*: "Auto-suggestion is a term which applies to all suggestion and all self-administered stimuli which reach one's mind through the five senses. Stated in another way, auto-suggestion is self-suggestion. It is the agency of communication between that part of the mind where conscious thought takes place, and that which serves as the seat of action for the subconscious mind."

There are three things to know about auto-suggestion:
(1) The mind automatically expresses an *accepted* idea;
(2) Your mind perceives every thought, every feeling, and every word as a suggestion; and
(3) The suggestions you persistently offer your mind shall eventually be accepted.

> An assumption, though false, if persisted in will harden into fact.
>
> - **Neville Goddard**

Advertisers understand this fact, which is why they spend billions annually to influence you. The Money Poems System teaches you to consciously influence your own mind. Through daily systematic repetition of the poems, you voluntarily create thought habits that condition you for wealth.

If you will change what you think, feel, and say, you will automatically change what you experience. No exceptions.

INTENSITY OF FEELING

Plain, unemotional words do not influence your mind. When you speak The Money Poems, do so with deep feeling. See the money you want coming into your experience. Feel the way you expect to feel when the money you desire manifests. Act like the words you speak have already been realized in your life.

> Determined imagination ... is the beginning of
> all miracles.

> **-Neville Goddard**

When Mark and I wrote the story of Denise Allen and her family, we wanted to create a narrative to show how the poems work in action. When Denise develops an intentional energy about using the poems, her results change. As her belief in the poems grew, the things she manifested expanded. The fiction of Denise's story does not diminish the principle: *words spoken with feeling manifest.*

The easiest way to put feeling behind your words is to make up your mind. When your mind is made up about a thing, the words you speak about it have definiteness to them. Think about a time when you have dug in your heels about a particular thing. It did not matter whether you were right or wrong about it; it was how you felt and nothing could convince you otherwise.

Nothing can stop the power of a made-up mind.

The other way to develop feeling for a thing is to think about it. Feelings follow thoughts. If you concentrate on a thing, you will find that your feelings for it will intensify over time. The Money Poems System gives you 7 times each day to concentrate positively on money. As you recite the poems throughout the day, you drum up positive feelings toward money.

One final way to intensify the energy behind the words of the poems is to write them down. When you write, you temporarily trap your concentration. Our minds cannot pay attention to anything else when we write other than to what we are writing. Only once you lift the pen, do you free the mind to wander again. Writing out the poems is an excellent way to intensify your feelings. Try it!

PERSISTENCE

No person becomes a saint in his sleep.

-Imelda Octavia Shanklin

Somewhere in the course of working The Money Poems System, you will experience resistance. It is not a question of *if*, it is a question of *when*. How and when that resistance appears varies from person to person. The question to answer today is *how will you respond?*

If you intend to develop true wealth—which The Money Poems can do for you—you must learn to push through your own internal resistance. In fact, your success with The Money Poems will be in direct proportion to your willingness to persist until your mind changes.

Resolve now to make The Money Poems System a non-negotiable part of your day. Just as you would not leave your home without brushing your teeth, organize your day so that you do not reach the day's end without working The Money Poems System.

We developed The Money Poems Tracker to help you. Our teacher, the Rev. Dr. Johnnie Colemon, taught us that "It works if you work it." The Money Poems Tracker will help you work it. Every day that you successfully recite the poems 7 times, put a star or check mark in the appropriate square. The natural tendency of the mind will be to complete a perfect tracker.

Persistence is an essential factor in the procedure of transmuting desire into its monetary equivalent … Lack of persistence is one of the major causes of failure.

-Napoleon Hill

One final note about persistence: Changing your character requires daily action. You really cannot let up on this thing. But you must be gentle with yourself. Work with a detached resolve; be determined but flexible. Weave The Money Poems System into the fabric of your life … gently.

It has been my experience that a small, doable daily discipline works best. In *The Slight Edge*, Jeff Olson explains: "The things you do every single day, the things that don't look dramatic, that don't even look like they matter, do matter. They not only make a difference-they make all the difference."

On the surface, The Money Poems do not look dramatic; they may even look like they don't matter. But they do. They make all the difference. They matter because life is not a linear endeavor. As Olson explains further, everything in life — in this universe — curves. The ground you stand on may appear flat, but it is not. And neither is anything else in the universe.

Your life curves, bending toward the things you do every single day. From where you stand today, it may be challenging to see the direction in which you are curving. But make no mistake, "we become what we do" (Will Coleman, PhD).

Your daily actions either curve you toward extraordinary success, or they curve you toward disappointing failure. Through persistent use, The Money Poems help you grow; over time, they curve you toward a life of health, happiness, prosperity, love, and abundance.

You cannot stand still in this universe. Grow, you must. That is the whole point of existence. That which ceases to grow, begins to die.

GRATITUDE

We live in a well-stocked universe. But you cannot take advantage of the opportunity you cannot see. And you certainly cannot benefit from the opportunity you don't know how to make use of. Gratitude—expressed gratitude—positions you to see opportunities that you could not see before, and it helps you maximize the opportunities you find.

We built a sense of gratitude into the language of each poem.

Gratitude has transformational power. It transforms whatever it is applied to. Don't take my word for it; experiment with it for yourself. For the next seven days, openly express gratitude to your spouse, significant other, sibling, parent, whomever … Journal your results so that you can look back over the week when you're done.

Gandhi once said, "Suffering cheerfully endured ceases to be suffering and is transmuted into an ineffable joy." Very often we remain locked in an unpleasant situation because we think our gratitude for something unwanted has no impact. It does. It transforms the situation; it transforms us.

Gratitude keeps you in tune with the Infinite and connected with the creative forces of the universe, and you become a mental and spiritual magnet attracting countless blessings.

-Dr. Joseph Murphy

Gratitude expressed does one of two things: (1) It turns what you have into something better so that you genuinely want it, or (2) it gently removes what you have from your life to make room for something better. For the longest time, I did not want to be grateful for the things I did not want because I thought my gratitude would lock those things into my life.

Now that I know the transforming power of gratitude, I often express it for things that someone else would be angry about. I know that enough gratitude expressed will transform what I don't want into something I do or remove it altogether.

THE MONEY POEMS TRACKING GRID

THE MONEY POEMS SYSTEM:

1. Recite the poem of the day with feeling 7 times during the day.

2. Keep this habit for 7 weeks and track your progress using The Money Poems Tracker on the next page.

3. Journal for 2 minutes daily on any insights that come up for you during this process.

4. At the end of the 7 weeks, assess your progress.

5. Repeat.

Every day that you successfully complete The Money Poems System, place a star in the square.

WEEK	SUNDAY	MONDAY	TUESDAY	WEDNES-DAY	THURSDAY	FRIDAY	SATURDAY
1							
2							
3							
4							
5							
6							
7							

EPILOGUE

It bears repeating that The Money Poems System does not replace taking action. Just as "faith without works is dead," using The Money Poems System without action is dead. What The Money Poems System does is slightly, often imperceptibly, tweak your actions. In the beginning, you probably won't notice much. But if you keep the journal as suggested, you will develop an eye for seeing the small incremental changes that happen in you when you take on the challenge.

We are made (or unmade) by the things we do every day. Adding The Money Poems System to your daily routine turns you into a magnet for wealth in all forms. More importantly, The Money Poems System helps you develop the consciousness for money. It moves you beyond a "by any means necessary," "grinding" and "hustling" mentality.

You cannot afford this kind of mentality because whatever you do to get a result will be *in* the result. In other words, whatever means you use to get what you want is that same thing you will experience once you have what you want. The end always matches the means; whatever is *in* the seed will be *in* the tree. If you begin with "I'm out here grinding" or "I'm hustling every day," then that is what you can expect in the end: a reality that you have to "grind" and "hustle" to maintain.

True prosperity includes peace of mind. The Money Poems System offers a different approach to wealth. You only "grind" and "hustle" when you do not know how to put yourself *in* the flow of universal abundance. The Money Poems System puts you *in* the flow. Applied faithfully, this system moves you peacefully from where you are today to a life filled with the riches of the universe.

We see you living the life you were born to live. We thank you for giving us an opportunity to share what our teachers have taught us. May your deepest and most heart-felt dreams find expression in you. May you always know that wealth is your birthright and you are extraordinary.

Richest blessings,

SHERRI JAMES   MARK ALLEN FELTON

Printed in Great Britain
by Amazon

22737215R00036